Visiting the **Dentist**

By
Joanna
Brundle

BookLife

©2017
Book Life
King's Lynn
Norfolk PE30 4LS

ISBN: 978-1-78637-069-3

Printed in Malaysia

A catalogue record for this book
is available from the British Library.

Written by:
Joanna Brundle

Edited by:
Grace Jones

Designed by:
Danielle Jones

Contents

What is a Dentist?

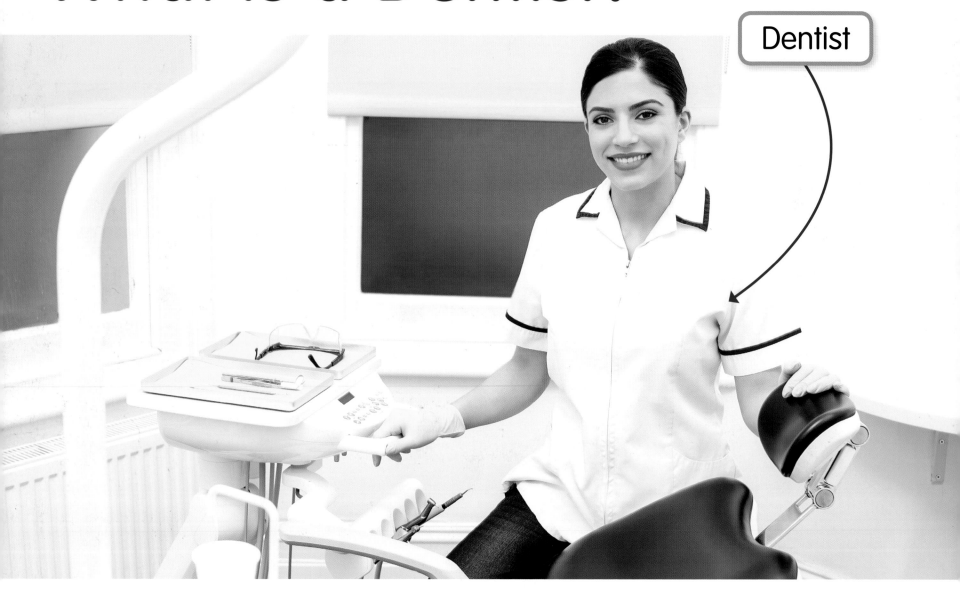

Dentist

Dentists are people who care for our teeth and gums.

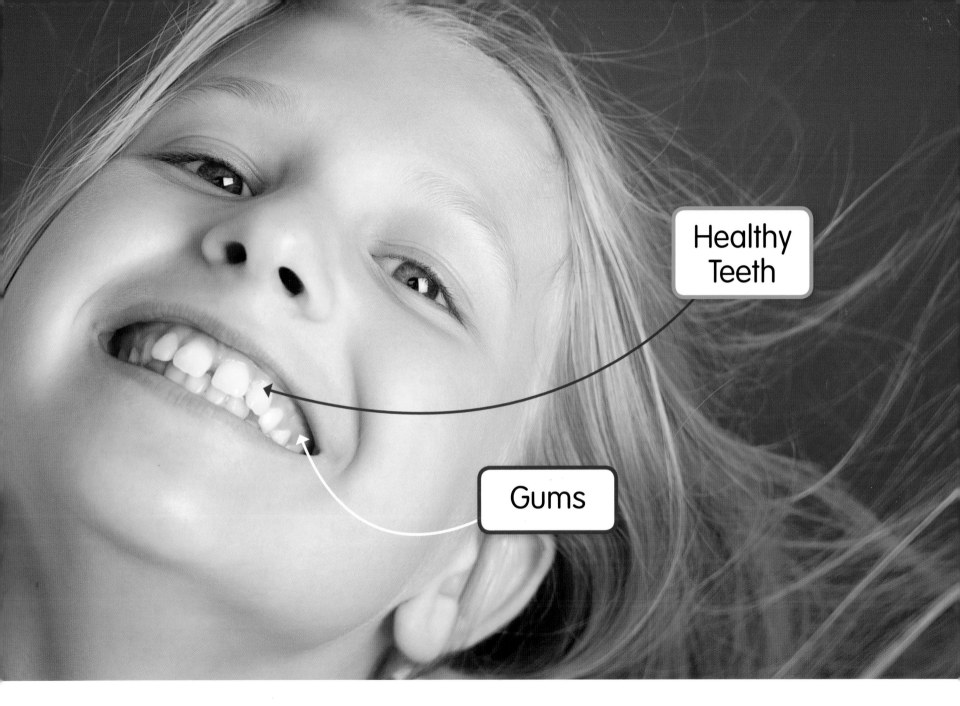

Healthy Teeth

Gums

Dentists help us to keep our teeth strong and healthy.

What are Teeth?

Biting and chewing

We need teeth to bite and chew our food.

We have milk teeth when we are children and adult teeth later.

Milk Teeth

Adult Teeth

Why do we Visit the Dentist?

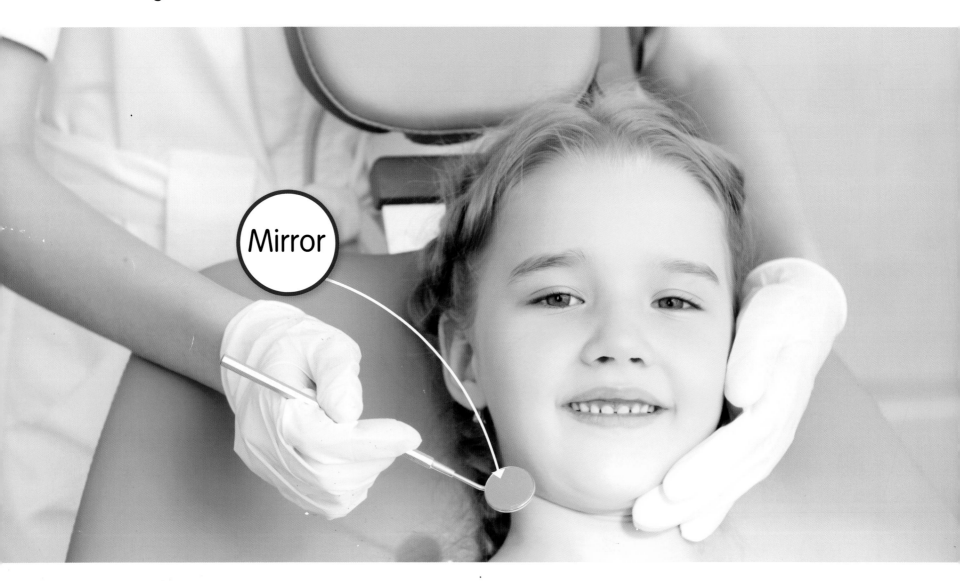

Mirror

The dentist uses a mirror to check our teeth. It doesn't hurt.

The dentist fills any holes with a special cream.

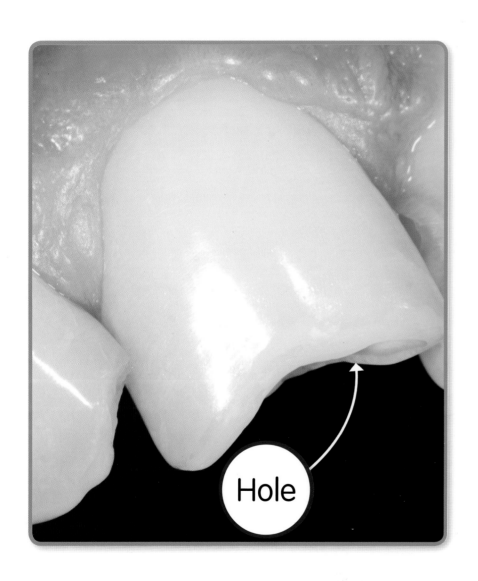

Hole

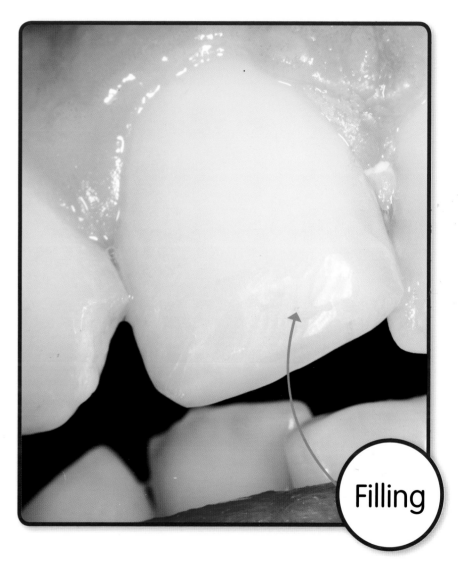

Filling

What Does the Dentist Look Like?

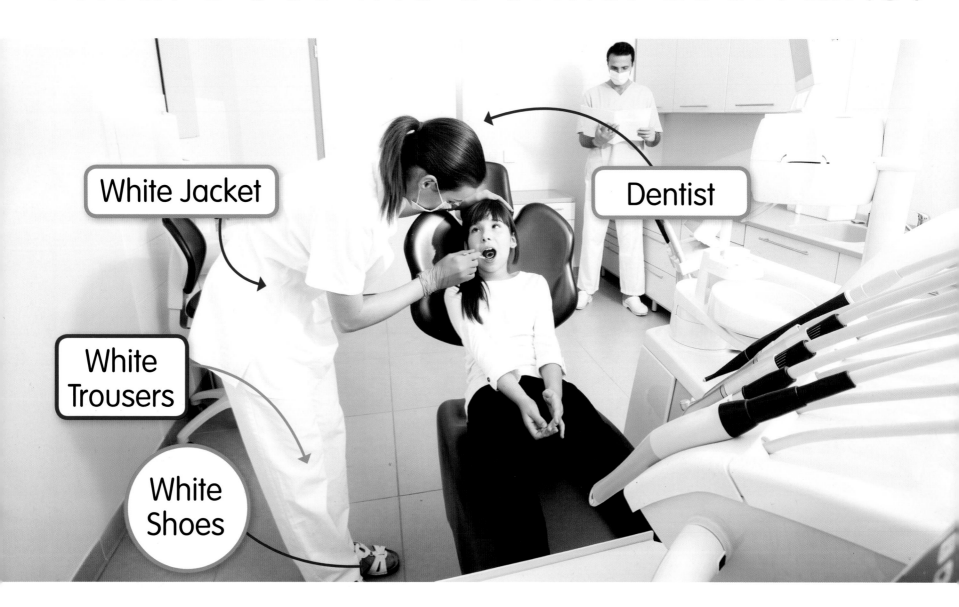

White Jacket

Dentist

White Trousers

White Shoes

The dentist and the dental nurse both wear a uniform.

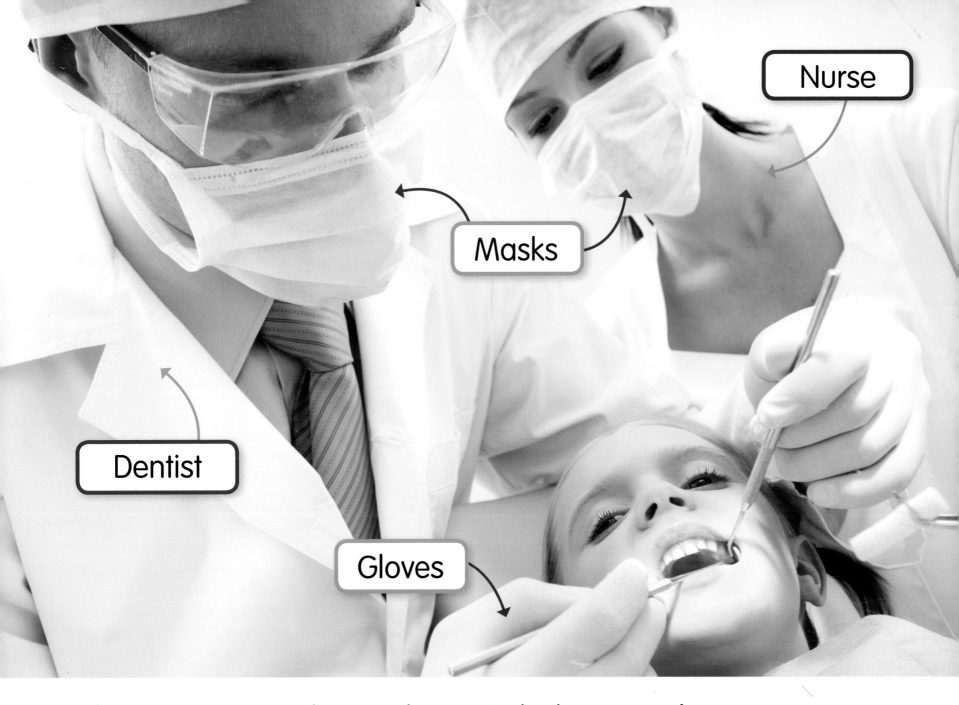

Nurse

Masks

Dentist

Gloves

They wear masks and special gloves to keep germs away from us.

The Dental Nurse

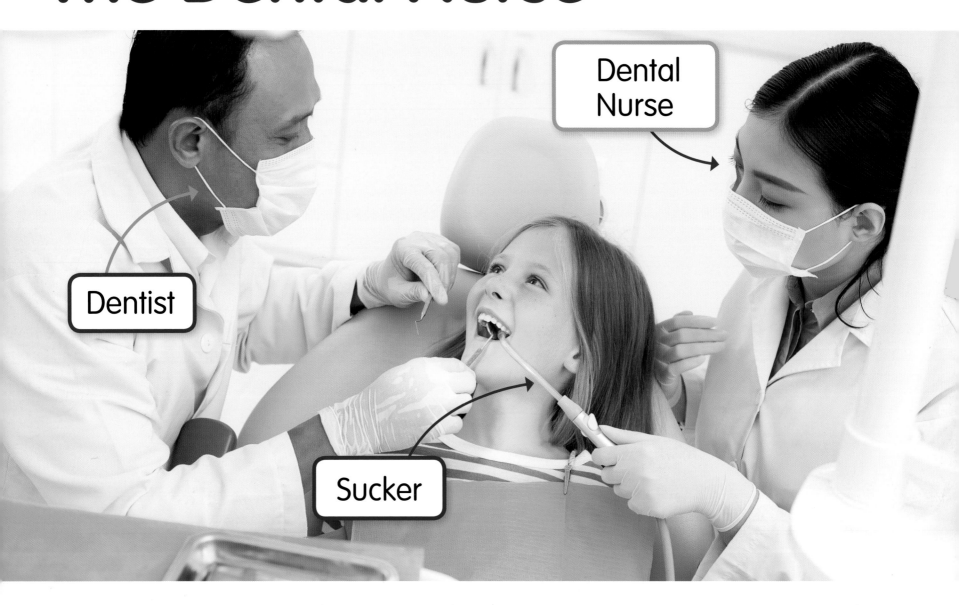

Dental Nurse

Dentist

Sucker

The dental nurse uses a sucker, so we don't dribble!

The dental nurse gives us a special drink to clean our mouth.

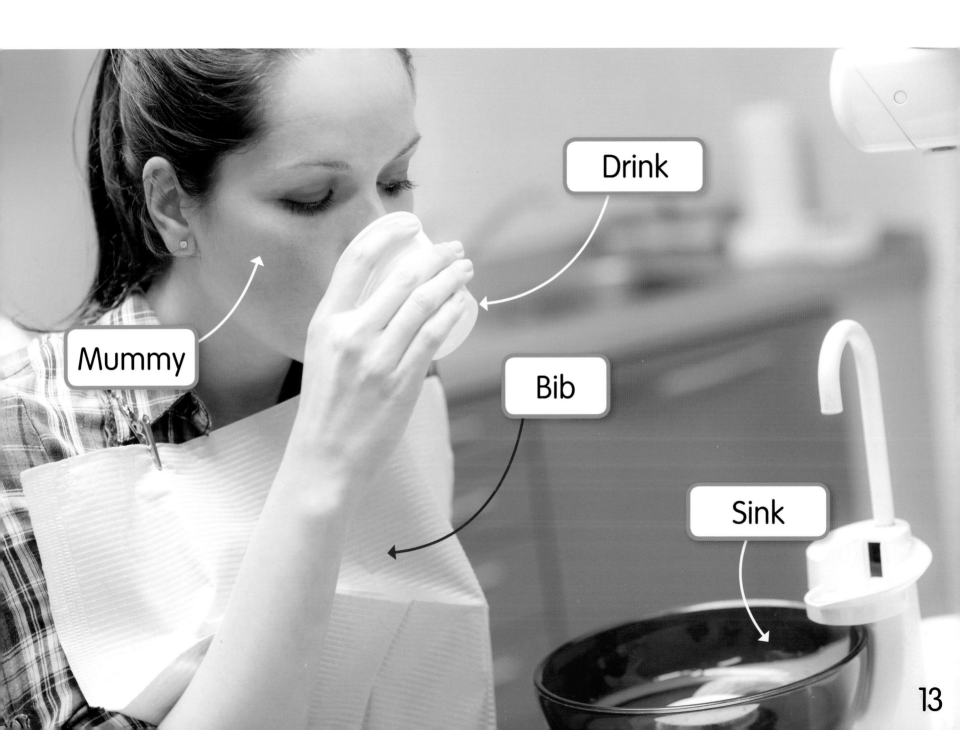

Mummy

Drink

Bib

Sink

13

Inside the Dentist's Room

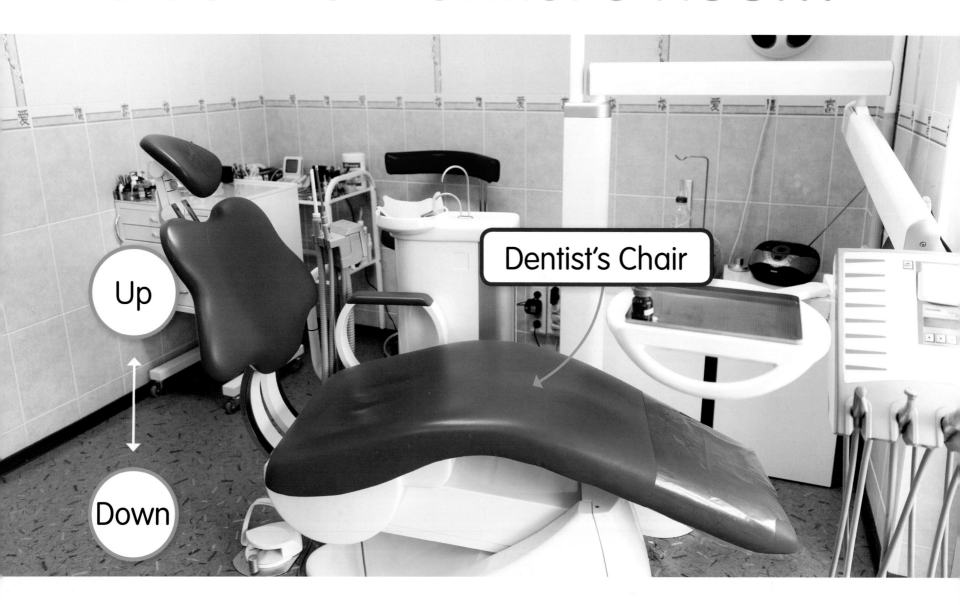

Up

Down

Dentist's Chair

A special chair tips back so the dentist can see our teeth.

It's dark inside our mouths! A big light helps the dentist to see our teeth.

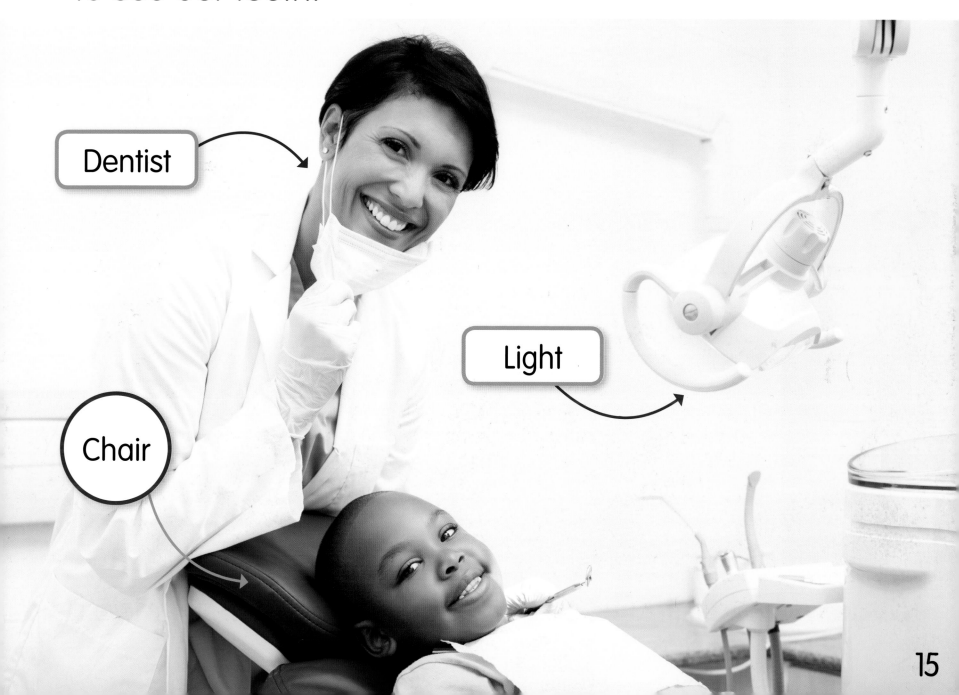

Dentist

Light

Chair

I Spy ...

Sugary drinks and sweets are bad for our teeth.

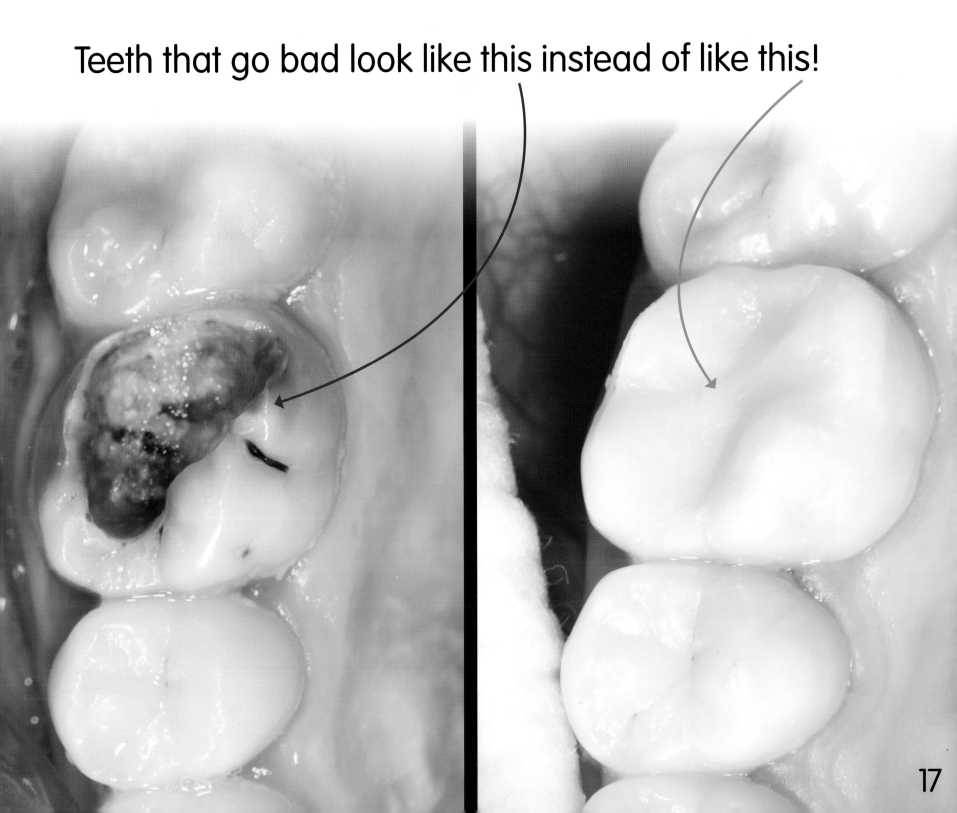

Teeth that go bad look like this instead of like this!

Having an X-ray

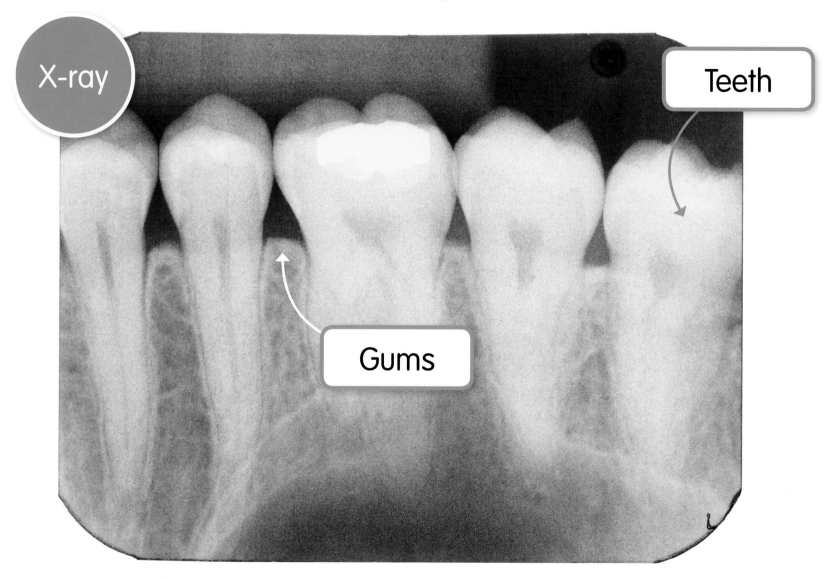

X-ray

Teeth

Gums

An X-ray shows the dentist how our teeth and gums look inside.

The X-ray machine looks like this.
We can't feel it working.

The Hygienist

Teddy comes too!

A hygienist helps us to keep our teeth very clean.

We learn how to brush our teeth properly.

Hygienist

Toothbrush

Pretend Teeth

Mummy

Going Home

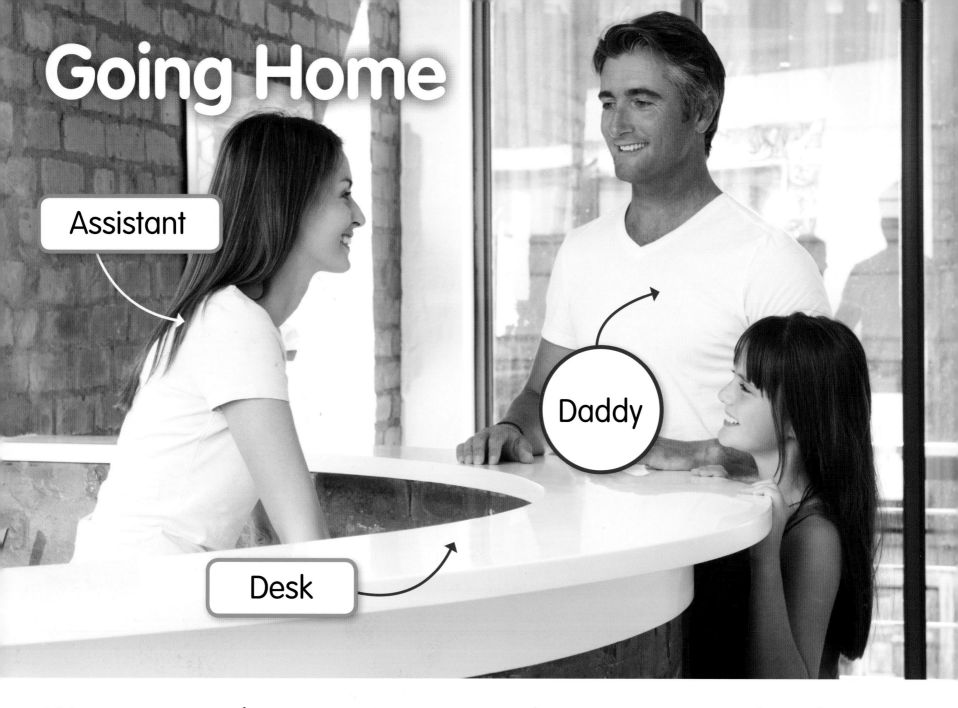

Assistant

Daddy

Desk

We arrange the next time we are going to visit the dentist.

At home, we must remember to brush our teeth twice a day.

Top Teeth

Toothbrush

Bottom Teeth

Index

Photo Credits

Abbreviations: l-left, r-right, b-bottom, t-top, c-centre, m-middle.

Front Cover l – Pressmaster. Front Cover ml – Kalmatsuy. Front Cover mr – Radharani. Front Cover r – Julia Metkalova. 1 – Lesya_boyko. 2 – Pressmaster. 3 – Brocreative. 4 – stockyimages. 5 – iconogenic. 6inset – Zurijeta 6 – Nina Buday. 7l – Radharani 7r – Rido. 8 – Khakimullin Aleksandr. 9 – Lighthunter. 10 – Spectral-Design. 11 – Pressmaster. 12 – Dragon Images. 13 – CandyBox Images. 14 – ET1972. 15 – wavebreakmedia. 16l – Marcos Mesa Sam Wordley 16r – Amelia Fox. 17 – botazsolti. 18 – chris kolaczan. 19 – Pavel L Photo and Video. 20 – gorillaimages. 21 – pikselstock. 22 – Monkey Business Images. 23 – Jiri HeraHands : racorn. Images are courtesy of Shutterstock.com. With thanks to Getty Images, Thinkstock Photo and iStockphoto.